THERE'S A CRICKET ON MY SHOE!

Poems for Boys

written by Lisa Benson Verner

Illustrated by Jason Kliewer

For Cohen Alexander

Copyright 2010

All rights reserved. This book may not be reproduced in any form without express written permission.

Published by
Cohen & Me PUBLISHERS

email: lisaverner@mac.com

Illustrations by Jason Kliewer
Typesetting by Julie Melton, The Right Type Graphics
Printed in the United States of America

ISBN: 978-0-615-36063-8
Library of Congress Control Number: 2010903655

There's A Cricket

There's a cricket on my shoe!
Now what am I supposed to do?
I'm so afraid that he'll fall off
I can't even sneeze or cough.
There's no way that this is fair,
he seems to be just sitting there.
I could scare him and do a dance
but he might jump up in my pants.
Oh, look at the time: it's getting late!
What do I do, just wait and wait?
Help! There's a cricket on my shoe!
Will someone tell me what to do?

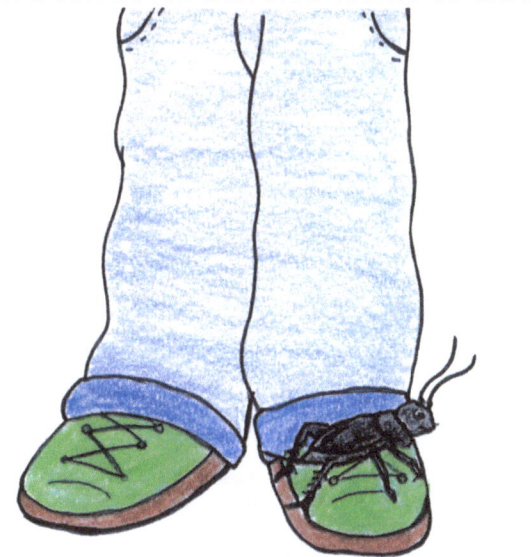

Dream On

I have a question if I might:
what happens if I don't sleep tight?
Will I wake up loose as a goose –
unable to sit or drink orange juice?

And just what if the bed bugs bite?
Will I not be able to write?
Must I only talk or sing:
walk around – my arm in a sling?

I wonder these things while in my bed
with covers pulled up over my head.
There's just too many risks to take
so maybe I'll just stay awake!

A Dog Tale

I think I'd like to have a dog –
not a cat or jumping frog.
He could watch me climb a tree
and always run along with me.
I might name him Blacky or Spot –
depends on what colors he's got.
I'll have to look in lost and found
or maybe the local doggy pound,
'cause I have no money to spend
on my newest, bestest friend.

Think

The sun is a hot circle up in the sky –
if you look at it – you'll burn your eye!
So use the brain that's in your head:
look at night at the moon instead!

A Dandelion

I blew on a dandelion today
and watched the seeds float away.
A few went up, up into the air –
then some landed in my hair.
Oops, one has landed on my toe –
it can't grow there, doesn't it know?

Gisa's Pond

I have to say I am quite fond
of throwing things in Gisa's pond!
Rocks, toys, a golf ball, a shoe
big and small, old or new.
In they go…splash, ker-plunk!
Down they go…sink, sank, sunk!

What to do?

Hey, what would you like to do?
It's your day; it's up to you.
There's always Monopoly, Scrabble or Clue
or how about crayons, paper and glue?
Say, we could put on just one shoe
and go outside and shoot a few.
What if we rode bikes to the zoo
to see the hyenas and porcupines too?
We could paint my door turquoise blue
but it's your day; it's up to you!

Counting 1 2 3

Can you count the stripes on a zebra,
spots on a cheetah?

Can you count the leaves on a tree,
sands by the sea?

Can you count the stars in the sky,
lashes on your eye?

These are all useless, surely you see,
so instead just count on me!

Shower Power

My mom's been saying for over an hour:
"Come inside and take a shower!"
Now, why is this such a must,
when I can't see a speck of dust
on any part of my clothes
or even between my littlest toes?
Not much I can do about this now
but let me tell you holy cow
I can't wait until I'm thirty –
I won't shower; I'll just stay dirty!

Family Tree

Mom says this photo is one of me
but it can't be true, how can it be?
This creature has no teeth or hair
and look – he has no underwear!

I have hair nearly to my chin
and people see teeth when I grin.
I'd never go anywhere without my clothes
and I think I'd remember sucking my toes!

So, sorry Mom but this can't be me,
he belongs on another family tree.

We Are

One inky, dark night Cohen and me
looked up to the sky and tried to see
the face on the moon and count the stars
but instead we saw how small we are.

Rock 'n Roll

Today I'm mostly still in shock
'cause yesterday I threw a rock
that flew a mile down the block
smacked Barry's dog named Socks
bounced off a painted fence
hit the neighbor boy named Vince
whose mom he's tried to convince
he hasn't seen his front tooth since!

Marshmallow Clouds

Hey, fat marshmallow up in the sky,

I love to watch you drifting by.

You are the fluffiest, whitest white.

Have you ever bumped a kite?

The most favorite thing I like to do

is fly in an airplane and look down on you!

A Fish Tale

If I could have just one wish,

I think I would like to be a fish.

Then I'd have fins instead of feet –

and no more broccoli would I eat!

Lizard

I saw a lizard on some rocks.

His feet were hot –

he had no socks!

He turned his head to look at me,

then scampered underneath a tree.

Tommy Thomas

My neighbor's cat Tommy Thomas
sat on the fence and looked at us.
He licked his face and looked around –
then made a funny meowing sound.
I told him we did not have a cat
but he still looked and that was that.

Girls

Girls are silly,
girls are pink.
Girls don't think the way I think.

Girls can play
but they won't.
If I chase them, they say don't.

Girls have friends
just like them
but that's ok, I'll play with him.

Mr. Tweedle VanZant

Hello there, little black garden ant,
tell me, is your name Mr. Tweedle VanZant?
I see you pushing a crumb with your nose –
The crumb is for dinner tonight I suppose?
You lift the crumb up over your head.
Why don't you just push it instead?
You disappear down a hole in the ground,
taking with you the treasure you found.
I wanted to watch you but now I can't –
where did you go, Mr. Tweedle VanZant?

Did You Know?

Did you know a palm tree has coconuts?

Drive a muddy road and you'll leave ruts?

That two monkeys like to share

or that a rabbit is a hare?

Feed Me!

The little brown bird begged for his dinner
'cause he swore he was much thinner
than he was just yesterday.
I fed him crumbs and had to say,
"My, my that was April and now it's May!"

Fast

I ride my bike fast up the street,

shiny pedals spin underneath my feet.

Wanna race? I can't be beat!

Ahhh, wind in my hair.

Look! My friend lives over there!

I'm riding my bike fast up the street.

www.ingramcontent.com/pod-product-compliance
Lightning Source LLC
Chambersburg PA
CBHW041234040426
42444CB00002B/163